GW01458616

Guitar Soloing Like a Pro

Book 1

Blue Morris

Written and Published in Vancouver, Canada

www.bluemorris.com

First Edition
ISBN 9798574100455
2 0 2 3 0 5 1 9

AUDIO AND VIDEO EXAMPLES

To download the audio samples for
Guitar Soloing Like a Pro Book 1
and other books by Blue Morris,
follow this link:

http://www.bluemorris.com/book-video

Table of Contents

Introduction

This book is for anyone who enjoys improvising or writing solos on the guitar, especially if you already know the pentatonic shapes but are tired of playing the same things all the time.

The truth is, there is so much more to guitar soloing than just the minor pentatonic scale. While you can play those five notes up and down the fretboard and in different octaves, it still only gives you five different sounds to choose from at any moment.

Sure there are hundreds of famous guitar solos in recorded history that use exclusively that scale, but it will restrict our creativity if it's the only method we know.

This book will help you gradually break out of that five-note "box." You will learn how to stop meandering around the scale and play with purpose. Soloing in music is all about making choices and the choices we make happen constantly throughout the song. It's more than just asking yourself what key a song is in.

Some of the choices we can make in solos:

Scale choices – Which scale do we start with? It's not just a matter of what key the song is in. We have options and we can select a scale that fits the song best, or fits the mood we want to present. (This book will work with the minor pentatonic and blues scales in detail. The next book will deal with major pentatonic and more.)

Changing scales, adding tones – Just because we started with one scale, doesn't mean we have to stick to that scale for the entire solo. We have many options to change scales or add notes at any point in our solos. Each chord in the song offers a new set options we can choose from.

Double Stops – Our solos don't always have to be played in single notes. We can use double stop licks to add texture to a solo. A double stop is when we play two notes at the same time. This gives us a bigger sound and adds harmony to our lines.

Chords – If we can play two notes at once, we can certainly play three or more at once. We can use chords higher up the fretboard in our solos to add even greater texture and larger sounds.

Targeting Chord Tones – The pentatonic scales don't include all the notes of the chords underneath. If there's a certain colourful note in the chord of the song, then we can add it back in to our solos thus expanding the number of notes we can use.

Arpeggios – If we can play chords up the neck in our solos, that means we can also outline the notes of those chords in interesting ways. We do this by memorizing chord shapes up and down the neck and memorizing specific arpeggio patterns based on those shapes.

> *These are just a few of the options we will look at in this book. Soloing is all about the choices we make – not just the choice we make at the beginning before the music starts – but the choices we make when each moment in the song changes, when each new chord comes along.*

Prerequisites

I've written this book so that students of all levels can read through and learn at their own pace. That being said, if you already know the minor pentatonic shapes, you'll be able to dive in and learn a lot faster.

If you're not there yet, don't worry. I'll make sure to include all the diagrams and instructions along the way so you won't be missing anything.

Here are a few things that will help greatly if you already know them:

- Names of the notes on the low E and A strings.

- Basic Minor pentatonic shape (first finger E string position)

- How to read tablature and chord grids

What you need to know to start this book

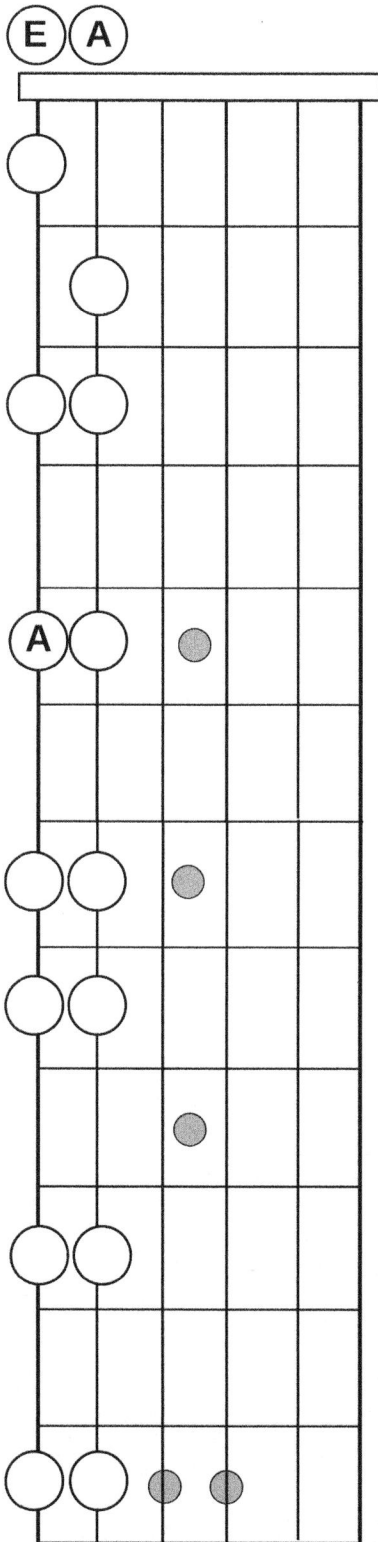

It will help you immensely if you memorize the notes on the low E and A strings. These are incredibly important because we are going to use the notes on these strings as landmarks for finding the scales and chord shapes we will play in this book.

If you have not spent the time to learn these yet, at the very least just know that the fifth fret of your low E string is A.

Since the fifth fret of the E string is A, then if we start our standard minor pentatonic shape from the fifth fret we will have "A Minor Pentatonic."

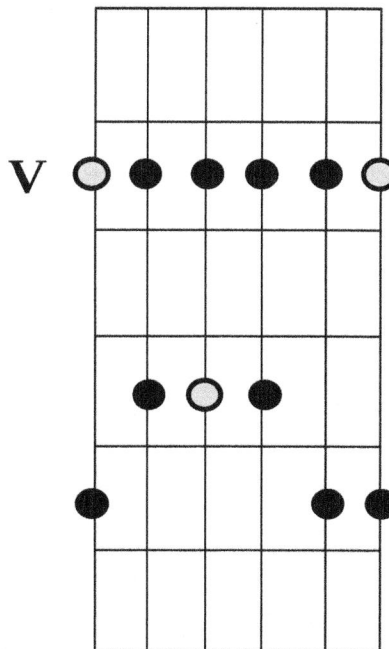

A Minor Pentatonic

Soloing in Zones

After teaching guitar for ten years I came up with many different ways to help students understand the fretboard. Most teachers will show students how to play the minor pentatonic shapes up and down the fretboard and indeed I do teach this way but only up to a point.

To really understand the fretboard we also need to imagine what else is in the vicinity of each pentatonic shape. I call these zones.

The purpose of this method is so that you can break out of playing the pentatonic "box" and have more creative options to choose from at any moment. We will start with Zone 1 Minor Pentatonic because that's the shape that most people learn first so you probably already know it.

Zone 1

Zone 1 – A Minor Pentatonic

I like to think of Zone 1 as the "First-Finger Low E String" shape because it starts on the low E string with your first finger on the root of the minor pentatonic scale.

Here is A Minor Pentatonic:

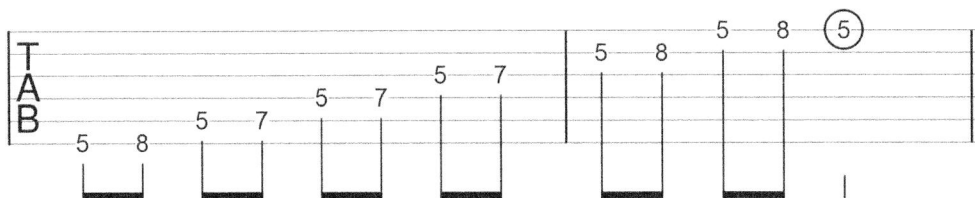

There are hundreds of famous guitar solos that were played exclusively in this shape. Zone 1 is great on guitar because it's comfortable to play and it's easy to reach all the notes we might want. It also feels logical because our first finger starts on the root note on the bottom string.

Here's another way to write that out. Notice that the root notes are highlighted with a lighter shade.

**Zone 1
for A Minor Pentatonic**

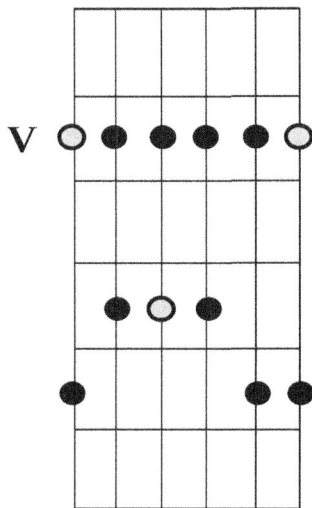

To get warmed up, let's try a few classic licks in this zone. If you've been playing guitar for a while, you have likely played these licks or similar ones in solos before.

Zone 1 Blues Scale

The pentatonic shape sounds great on its own, but since it's only five notes it is rather limiting. So let's add the **blue note** to the Zone 1 Shape. Sometimes this is called the **blues scale**, or sometimes the **minor blues scale**. It is essentially just the minor pentatonic scale with the blue note added.

```
T|------------------------------------------|---------------------5--8--5--|
A|----------------------------5----|----7--8----5--8----------|
B|--5--8----5--6--7----5--7----------|------------------------------|
       ⌐⌐   ⌐⌐   ⌐⌐   ⌐⌐       ⌐⌐   ⌐⌐   ⌐⌐
```

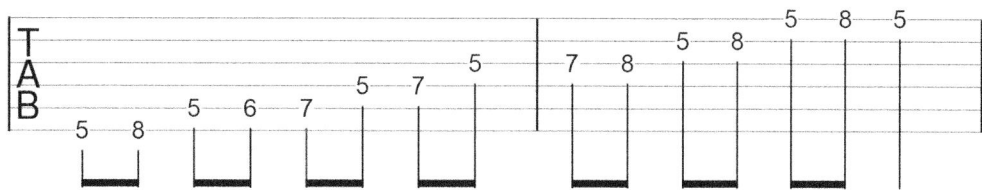

In the diagram below I have indicated the blue note with a "B" so you can remember where it is visually. While it's important to memorize the shape as a whole, we should also remember specifically where our roots are and where the blue notes are. That way we can use the shapes in a more intentional way.

**Zone 1
for A Minor Blues**

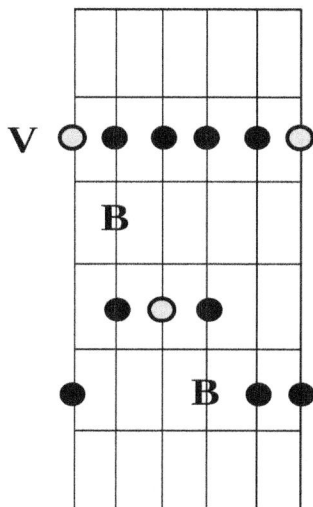

Here are some common licks using the Zone 1 blues scale. Notice that we don't tend to hold on to the blue note for long. Because the note is so dissonant, we generally want to walk through it, or up to it and away from it.

②

Common Notes to Bend in Zone 1

Rather than guessing at which notes will sound good to bend in your solos, we can categorize them so you'll always know where they are and which ones will give you the flavour you are looking for.

Bend 3rd Finger G-string

One of the most common bends in this pentatonic shape is the third-finger G string bend.

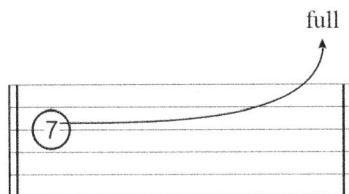

In the key of A minor, that means we are bending the D note, the 4th degree of the full minor scale. Knowing this helps us to understand that we can bend that note up a whole step, raising the pitch to become the fifth of the scale.

In short, this note is great to bend because it tends to resolve. It's a good way to end a phrase, especially when played over the root I chord.

Bend to the Blue Note

We can also bend that note a half-step in pitch and it will give us the sound of the blue note (D becomes D#). Generally speaking, when we bend to the blue note we don't want to hold that pitch for long. The blue note is dissonant (in a good way), but we typically want to resolve that dissonance soon after.

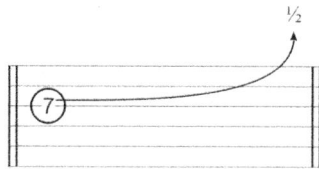

The next example demonstrates the different ways to bend that note in the context of the minor pentatonic scale. Notice that the first time we bend that note, it's up a whole step. The second time it's just a half-step up to the blue note. And indeed we don't hold it as long as the others since that note will want to resolve pretty quick.

③

B and E String Bends

The other common places to bend in this zone are the 8th fret of the B string and 8th fret of the high E string. While we might commonly use the pinky finger to play these notes, if we're setting up for a bend it's common to use the 3rd finger so we have more strength. We can also add in the first and second fingers below for extra support, effectively bending the string with two or three fingers.

④

Another thing to consider about these bends is that you can always repeat the note unbent before or after the bend. Notice in measure three above, we bend the 8th fret and then we play the 8th fret unbent. This is a common effect and sounds great.

Memorize where these common notes to bend are. The easiest way to do that is to visualize them in the pentatonic shape – they are circled in the diagram below.

Common Notes to Bend in Zone 1

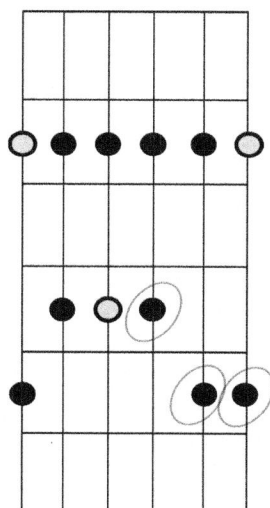

Types of Bends

Many students who come to me for lessons only tend to think of bends in one manner: just bend it up and hear what happens. But there are actually three different types of bends we can do and if you listen to solos by the guitar greats you will certainly hear all these techniques at different times.

Bend and release – This is the most intuitive type. Bend the note up to the desired pitch, then relax the string so we hear the note descend back to its original pitch.

Bend up only – What goes up does not necessarily have to come down. We can bend the string up and hold it at the desired pitch, then mute the string with our right hand as we release the bend with our left hand. That way we don't hear the note descend because the string has been stopped with our right hand.

Pre-Bend – Before you pluck the string, bend it up with your left hand, then pluck the string. After it's plucked, gradually release the bend. You have to "guess" how hard to bend it because you won't be able to hear the pitch until after you've plucked the string. With some practice you can nail a whole-step pre-bend.

> *Listen for the pre-bend in the intro to the Beatles' song "Something," and on Eric Clapton's solo in "While My Guitar Gently Weeps." The pre-bend is perfect for that "crying" or "wailing" sound.*

In tablature, the type of bend is usually indicated by the shape of the arrow. Compare these three examples below. The first is a regular bend-then-release. The second is a bend without release, the third is a pre-bend.

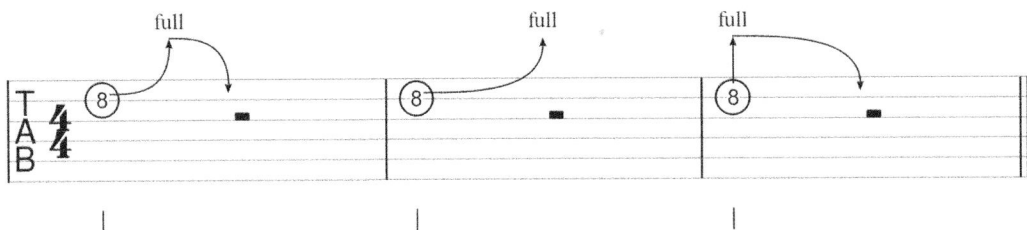

> *Sometimes tablature will have the letters "pre" over top as further indication that you should pre-bend the note before plucking it.*

Here's a short exercise using these different types of bends. Just examine carefully the arrows indicating what type of bend it is. For example, the bend in bar three is a pre-bend.

Pattern 1 – Up 4 Back 1

Since we tend to practice scales ascending and descending the notes in order, we develop the habit of doing the same thing when we are improvising solos. But if too many of our lines are scale-wise, they can start to sound dull after awhile.

One way to make your playing more interesting is to make jumps, or skip around the scale shape a little. Large jumps can sound cool, but if you do too many large jumps it can sound too quirky. Ultimately, we want to create new habits of playing by practising patterns that aren't scale-wise. If these patterns become habitual, then you will play them while barely thinking about it.

I call this particular pattern "Up 4 Back 1" because you ascend four notes of the scale and then track back one step.

⑥

```
  5  8
T 4/4
A
B         5  8    5  7  5  7       5  7                    5  7  5  7          5  8       5  8         5     8    ⑤
                             5  7                                                                    
```

```
  8  5
T         8  5  8  5
A                        7  5       7  5                                7  5                    7  5
B                                            7  5  7  5               7  5                    8  5  8  5
```

There are hundreds of patterns out there and I don't necessarily recommend you learn them all. We will do a couple of my favourite patterns in this book. Practice them until they become a part of your usual playing style. When the pattern becomes natural to you, start using pieces of it in your solos.

> *If you play long pieces of the pattern in a solo it can sound too mathematical in my opinion. But when you play smaller pieces of the pattern and connect it with other licks, like bends or slides, now you've got something cool.*

Below are some examples of licks that begin by using the pattern, but end with a more melodic lick.

⑦

Blues Double Stops

When playing exclusively single-note lines, our solos can sound too thin after a while. To change that, we can add double-stops to our solos. Playing two notes at the same time adds thickness and excitement to a solo.

There are a few ways of achieving double stops. The most common is to play them in a blues style, like the example below. Variations of this lick have been used in countless blues and rock songs. Here's an easy example to get you started.

⑧

To remember where these double-stops are found, just memorize them based on the Zone 1 minor pentatonic shape. Notice that one of the notes is not in the minor pentatonic scale (7th fret of the B string). That's okay if it doesn't belong in the pentatonic -- it still sounds good!

**Zone 1
Blues Double Stops**

Here's a more complex rhythm that includes a lot more repetition of the double stops. This can be effective for the ending of a solo when you might want to build up to a bigger sound.

Jam Track 1

Now is your opportunity to try out these first concepts on a jam track. Play Jam Track 1 on speakers that are loud enough that you can play along to it on your guitar.

If you haven't already done so, you can download all the tracks from my website: **www.bluemorris.com/book-video**

Practice playing the following licks in time to the track. Once you can do that, start mixing and matching them in a different order. If that gets easy, try creating your own variations by changing the rhythms or adding notes from the minor pentatonic scale.

Anticipation

You can turn a simple lick into a more exciting lick simply by starting a note early, usually on the last eighth note (or up-beat) of the bar. If you look at the next exercise, you'll see the bend in the first measure does just that. It starts just before the second measure.

Anticipation is especially common with bends but of course you can use it with any line. It can make your solo sound like it is pushing forward, or that the notes just can't wait to get out.

A good example of this is the solo on ACDC's "You Shook Me All Night Long." Angus Young plays a number of anticipated bends -- not the one that starts the solo, but several others throughout.

⑪

Doubling Notes

One of my favourite techniques is fairly easy to master and it can turn any simple pentatonic line into something interesting. All you need to do is play the scale but occasionally hit a note twice. You can do this almost randomly. It doesn't matter which note you double. Just try to do it whenever you think of it.

I find this sounds especially good at higher tempos. I started using this technique more when I noticed how often Mike McCready from Pearl Jam does this on the solo of "Alive."

To get you warmed up for doubling notes, try playing the scale up and down with each note played twice. Once you can play this at a high tempo, you should be ready for the next exercise.

Now let's put this into practice. Try getting this next exercise up to 180 beats per minute. Use a metronome or play along to the recording which you can download from my website.

As an additional tip, if you want to use this technique at slower tempos, just hit the notes as sixteenth notes (play them twice as fast as the other notes that come before and after).

Soloing Over Chords

One sure sign of sounding amateur is to solo away without considering the chord changes underneath. Too many students don't think much about the chords they are soloing over. They just determine what key the song is in and just blast away from there. That can work for a lot of songs with simple chord changes that stay in key, but we are missing out on a lot of harmonic colour and loads of great tricks.

From now on, your goal is to consider all the chords that are played under the solo. Start listening to the harmonic changes of the song as you solo. Each chord gives us a new opportunity to alter what we are playing.

> *Don Felder's guitar solo in Hotel California is a great example of targeting notes that come from the chord changes underneath. Right in the third bar of his first solo, listen to him hit that unique note that is totally outside the pentatonic shape, but so perfect for the chord underneath.*

Targeting the roots of the chords

In this example we are going to solo over just two chords: Am and Dm -- two measures of each. Here's the outline:

    | Am | Am | Dm | Dm |

Using A minor pentatonic, we could solo over the first two bars playing any licks we like, but when the Dm chord happens we could target the D note of the scale since that's the root of the Dm chord.

So in bar three, we could hit a single D note and just let it ring over that D minor chord. It will highlight that chord perfectly and help to anchor the sound of your solo in the chord change.

Targeting Exercise

Below is an exercise that will help you practice this. Notice that the first note of bar 3 is the root of the Dm chord (D on the 5th fret of the A string). In bar 5 the song returns to the Am chord so we hit the root of Am (the A note on the 5th fret of the low E string).

Then again, in bar 7 when the song switches to Dm for the second time, we hit another D note, this time up the octave (D on the 7th fret of the G string).

By playing the roots on the chord changes, we highlight the chords of the song. We don't have to do this every time, but it is a great trick for making your solos sound more melodic.

Jam Track 2 – Am to Dm

This simple jam track was designed for you to try targeting the roots of these two chords whenever the changes happen. Keep your solo simple at first. If you find it difficult to hear the chord changes, just play very basic lines and try to hit a root note on each chord change.

Chords for Jam Track 2:

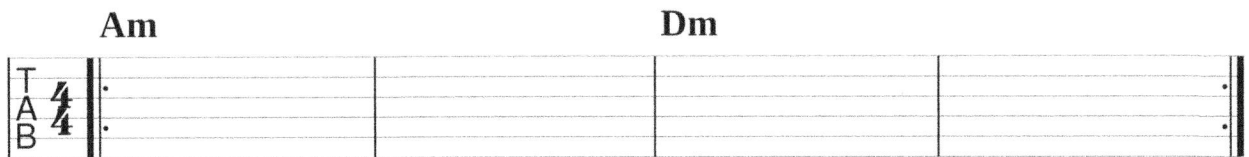

I and IV chords

We need to get a little theory out of the way before we can take this to the next level. So let's review what is meant by a "IV chord." It's quite simple really: If Am is the root chord of the key, then the Am chord would be the I chord. From there, each chord gets a number (indicated in roman numerals):

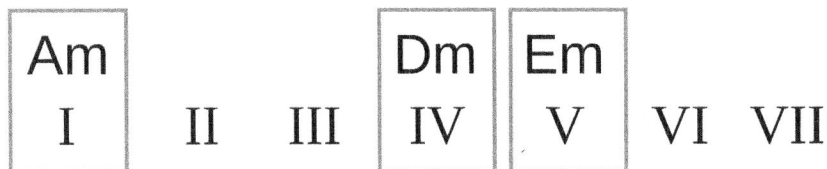

Don't worry about all the details if this diagram looks unfamiliar to you. Just know that **each chord gets a number, so if Am is the I chord, then Dm is the IV chord**.

Targeting the Minor 3rd of the IV chord

In the last example we practised targeting the root notes of each chord. In this case, we're going to target a very specific note that sounds magical when you get it right. It's the minor 3rd of the IV chord.

That sounds complicated but it's not difficult if you just memorize where this special note is. In the key of A minor, the I chord is Am and the IV chord is Dm. So let's look at the Dm chord shape:

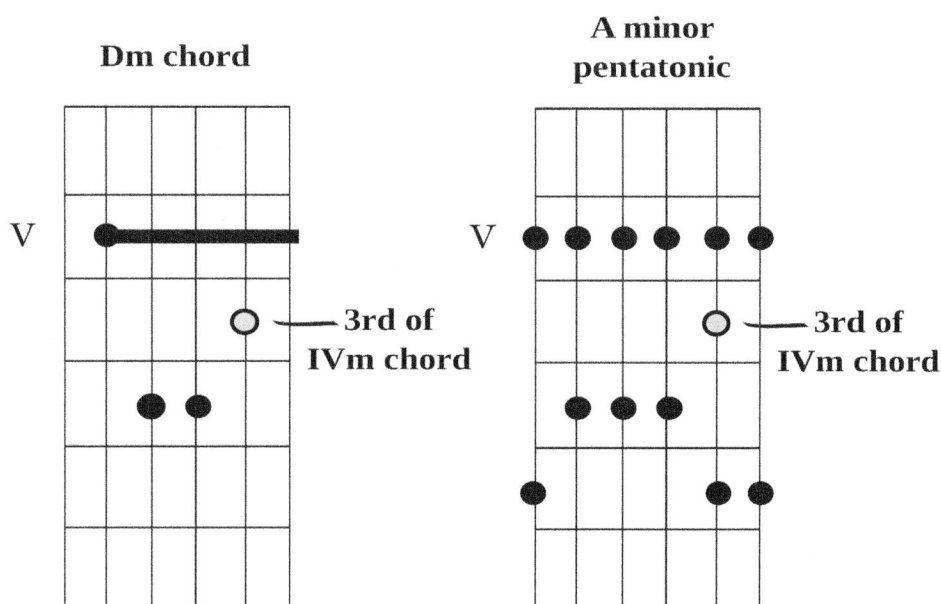

Dm chord

A minor pentatonic

— 3rd of IVm chord

— 3rd of IVm chord

The first diagram above shows you where that 3rd is in the Dm bar chord shape. Memorize where that note is because anytime a song is on a Dm chord we can play that note. All we have to do is picture this chord shape, target that note, and just let it sing.

We can also picture where it sits in relation to the minor pentatonic scale, as we see in the second diagram above.

Notice that this special note isn't in the A minor pentatonic scale. That's good news in a way because it will come as a beautiful surprise when we play it at the right moment. We can use it whenever a song is on a IVm chord and we can let that note ring out in all its harmonic glory.

This next exercise is similar to the last one, but instead of hitting the root of Dm, we aim for the minor 3rd.

Once you have the idea down, go back to Jam Track 2 and try them out with your own improvised lines, aiming that minor 3rd for the Dm chord.

Minor Over Major

In rock, and especially in the blues, we are often playing A minor pentatonic (or the blues scale) over a series of major chords. It's possible that you didn't even notice the discrepancy because it's so common. There are millions of rock songs that have chords like A, D, and E (all *major* chords) but we have blasted into a **minor** pentatonic solo over those **major** chords.

Theoretically, this should not sound good. If the underlying chords are all *major*, why would we play a *minor* scale over them? Part of the reason why it works is because the pentatonic scale only has five notes so we avoid some notes that will conflict.

But that's not the only reason. We are still left with a minor 3rd in the scale while the major chord underneath has a major 3rd. Despite this conflict, it just sounds cool. The blues players have been doing it for about a hundred years now and our ears are accustomed to it.

Major 3rd of the I chord

If the song is in a major key, then the I chord will have a major third. Again, this particular note is not in the minor pentatonic scale. But since it's in the chord underneath we can play it anytime that the I chord comes around.

> *Here's a rule of thumb: If the notes are in the chord underneath, we can use them, even if the notes are not in the scale we've chosen to play.*

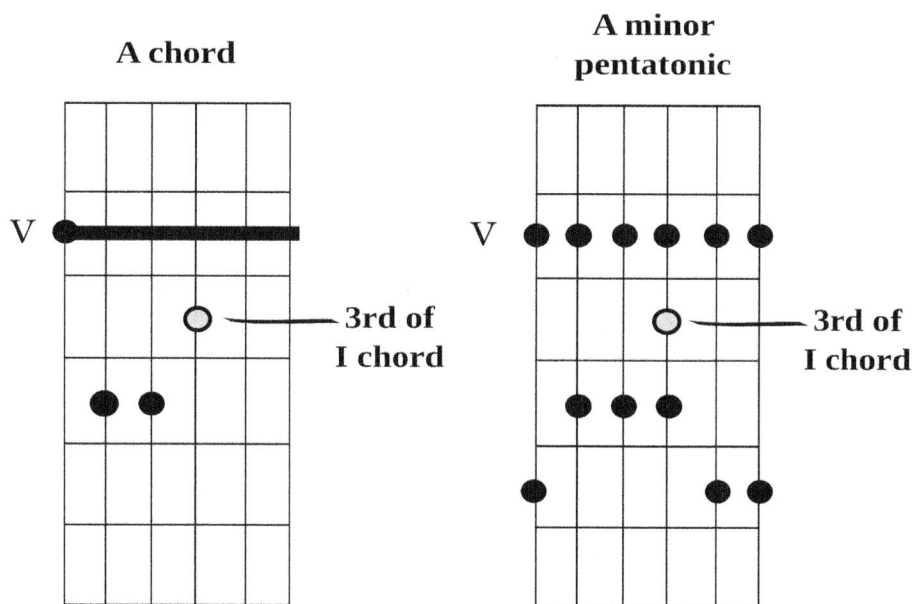

The first diagram above indicates where that 3rd is in the A major bar chord shape. Memorize where that note is and all you have to do is picture this chord shape to target that note when the song is on an A major chord.

Notice that this special note isn't in the A minor pentatonic scale. Again, that's good news because it will come as a nice surprise when we play it at the right time.

This exercise is reminiscent of 50s rock and roll, as the likes of Chuck Berry used this trick a lot in his solos. Whenever there's an A chord, we make use of its major 3rd, usually by approaching it from one fret below.

Major 3rd of the major IV chord

Similarly, if the song is in a major key, then the IV chord will also have a major third. Again, this particular note is not in the minor pentatonic scale. But since it's in the chord underneath we can play it anytime that IV-major chord comes around.

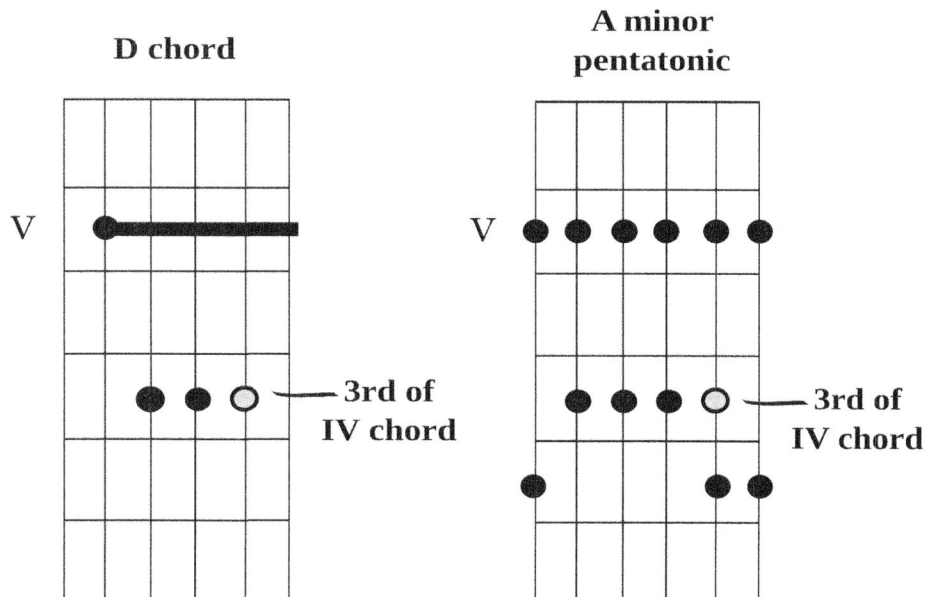

D chord

A minor pentatonic

V

3rd of
IV chord

V

3rd of
IV chord

The above diagram indicates where that 3rd is in the D major bar chord shape. Memorize where that note is and all you have to do is hit that note when the song is on an D chord.

The next exercise will help you practice targeting this note. Notice that in bar three as the song switches to a D chord, all we do is hit that major third of the D chord and let it sing the whole bar.

This next exercise is a slow blues in 6/8 time, so the rhythmic pulse is in groups of six. Think: **1** *2 3* **4** *5 6*

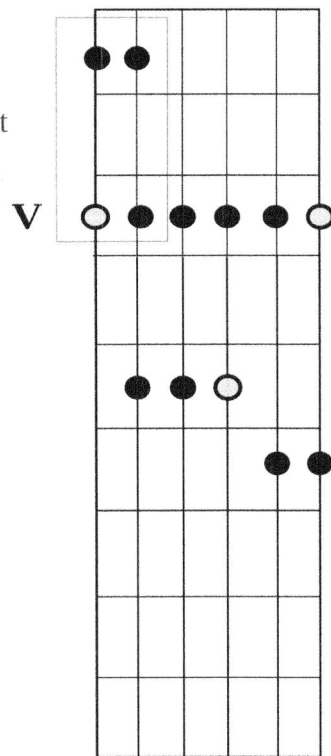

Runs

So far, most of this book has discussed note choices based on only one shape of the minor pentatonic scale and on chord shapes in that area. Now we are going to expand your Zone 1 Minor Pentatonic shape so that we can play longer **runs**, or longer lines of single notes. If you know your pentatonic shapes well, these runs may look familiar to you.

Lower Section Runs

First we will start by adding some notes that are lower in pitch, just below the A root we were starting on previously.

17

Notice that we no longer start on the root note when we play this run. The root is the second note we play. I've off-set that first note so that the root note lands on a down beat.

This lower section of Zone 1 works especially well for ascending through a long run of single notes. It's also used as an alternative way to end a line and resolve on the root. The following exercise achieves both of these things.

18

Upper Extension Runs

There is a very common way to travel up the fretboard to higher notes that some people call **the box**. The problem with this term is that some people call other shapes the box. I tend to call this one the **extension** to avoid this confusion.

More importantly, this extension shape is where tons of classic licks happen. In just one small shape we can get all five notes of the pentatonic scale neatly tucked all together.

This next exercise demonstrates how to play the entire run – from the new lower section down at the 3rd fret, all the way up to the extension as high as the 10th fret. Memorize this run because you can use it when you want a long line in any of your solos. You could even add the blue note in when you want.

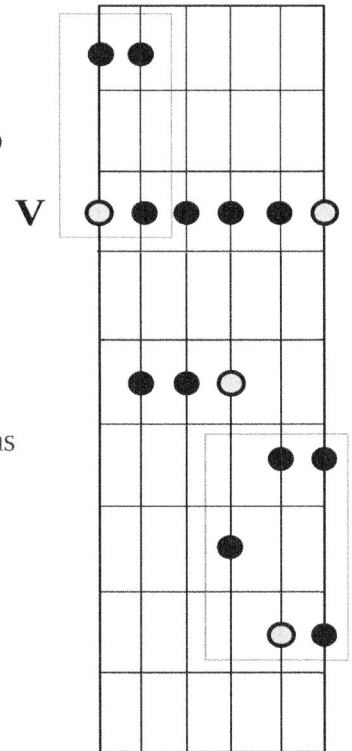

Blues Example with the Extension Shape

The following exercise uses both the lower and the upper extensions of Zone 1. It incorporates lots of the things you've learned so far including the minor pentatonic shapes, the blue note, good places to bend, runs, and the extensions.

> *Notice that the 10th fret of the high E string is an excellent sounding note for bends. Add this to your memorized places for good bending notes*

⑳

Pattern 2 – Up 3 Back 1

Here's your next pattern to work on. If you master these patterns you will be able to play these shapes smoothly, quickly, and they will inform your improvising in creative ways. I call this "Up 3 back 1" because you ascend three notes, track back one note, then continue on three notes from there.

(21)

More Double Stops

There's another important double-stop lick that we should all learn and it's in the extension shape that you find at the top of the Zone 1 Run.

**Zone 1
Extension Double Stop**

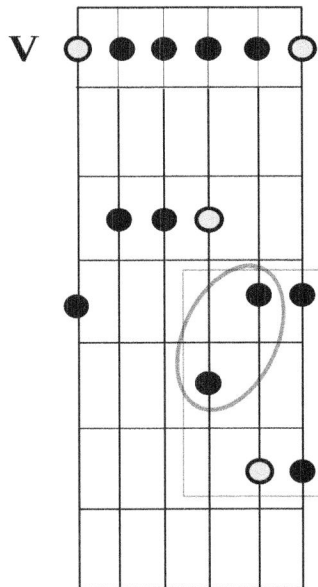

This double-stop was used often by electric blues players and you can hear it on countless recordings. Below is an exercise that will help you practice this double-stop and combine it with the others we have already learned.

Blue Note in the Upper Extension

There's another location to play the blue note at the top of our extension shape in Zone 1. This is such a great spot for it because it becomes the highest point we play in this shape. It's perfect for those "touch and go" blue-note licks.

The blue note is indicated with a bold letter "B" in the diagram below.

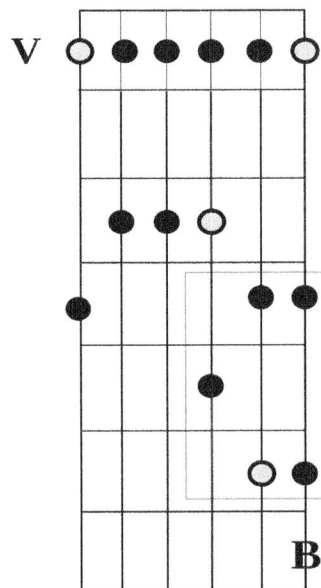

Here's an example of the kind of "touch and go" trick I like to use this blue note for. This exercise is played entirely within the extension shape. Sometimes we only need a few notes to make a great solo. Indeed this next exercise is inspired by the sound of B.B. King who could make an incredible solo out of just one small area of the fretboard, making great use of bends, vibrato, and the blue note.

Notice in bar seven we bend the 10th fret a whole step, then a half-step to the pitch of the blue note.

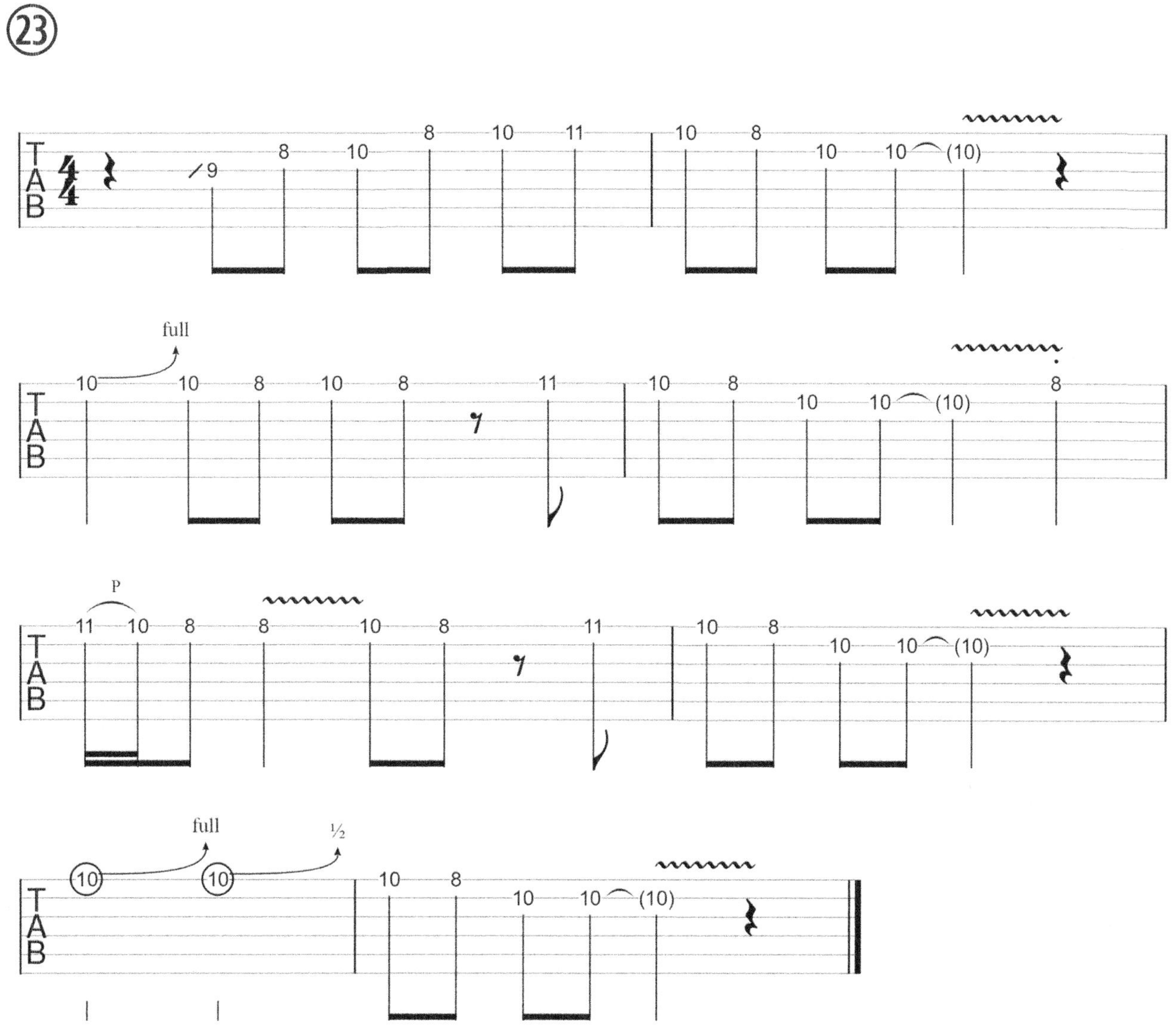
23
T
A
B
full
P
½

Chords for Solos in Zone 1

Now that we're learning to hear the chord changes when we solo, we can explore how to play small chords in this zone. If you're going to play a chord in a solo, it's usually best to play them on the higher strings. Otherwise, the lower pitch chords don't punch through the mix like a high-pitched chord can.

The best way to start playing chords in solos is to memorize where your I, IV and V chords are in this zone. These are the most common chords we find in popular music so it's the best place to start.

I-IV-V in A Minor

First, let's review what the three chords are in A Minor. The key of A Minor conveniently has no sharps or flats, so the available notes are A B C D E F and G. The chords available are:

Chords in A Minor

Am	Bdim	C	Dm	Em	F	G
I	II	III	IV	V	VI	VII

Therefore, the three most common chords in A Minor are:

I: Am   IV: Dm   V: Em

The following charts show the standard bar chord forms. I find that these shapes can be too big and clunky for solos. The second row illustrates the shortened chord forms that use just the high strings. Notice how these "soloing chord forms" are just smaller versions derived from the standard bar chord shapes. Recognizing them this way makes it easier to memorize them.

Standard bar chord forms

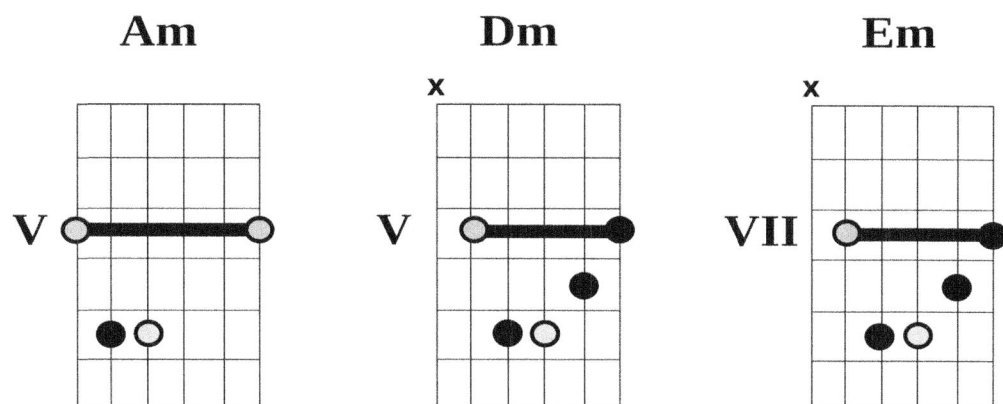

Soloing chord forms

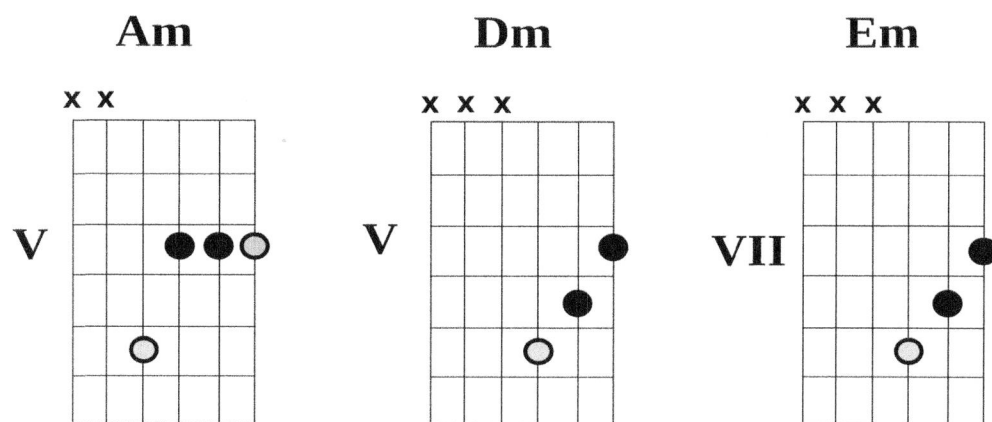

Here's an example of how we can use the Am chord mixed in with some minor pentatonic lines.

Now let's try putting some other chords into the mix. Generally speaking, you should only use these chords when the underlying chord in the song is the same at that moment. So if the song is currently on a Dm chord, you would use the Dm chord in your solo. If you play the Em shape over a Dm chord it may not sound as you expect it would.

Here's a short example that starts with the same four bars as above, but then shifts to Dm, back to Am, and eventually to Em.

Jam Track 3 – Thirds and Chord Licks

Try writing or improvising a solo over Jam Track 3. You have many different tools you can use now. Try anticipation, double-stops, and bends. Aim for a chord tone such as the minor 3rd of Dm. Or try hitting any of the "soloing chord forms" at the appropriate time. Take note of the chord structure of the Jam track before you begin and listen for the changes when you're playing.

Chords for Jam Track 3:

Arpeggios

Now that you have some soloing chord forms on hand from the previous chapter, you can also use these shapes to play arpeggios in your solos. An arpeggio is essentially just the notes of a chord played one at a time, rather than strummed. The good news is that we can use those same three chord shapes from before. The arpeggios based on those shapes would look like these ones below.

Notice that the D minor arpeggio has a note that isn't in the A minor pentatonic scale. Remember this is just because the pentatonic scale has only five of the notes from the full seven-note scale. Regardless, if the note is being played in the chord by the rest of the band, that note is certainly fair game.

Below is an exercise that will help you connect the arpeggios with the A minor pentatonic scale. Every note is an eighth-note so try to play them as evenly as possible without any breaks.

Arpeggio Licks

Here are some licks that integrate these arpeggios along with the minor pentatonic scale. Notice how the arpeggios highlight the sounds of the chords they are outlining. Arpeggios are a great way to make certain moments in your solos "jump out" because they highlight the harmony of the underlying chords.

Repeat Jam Track 3 with arpeggios

Now try going back to Jam Track three and use it to practice these arpeggio shapes. Connect the shapes with the A minor pentatonic scale and be sure to listen for the chord changes on the track so you're certain to play the corresponding arpeggio at the right time.

Extending the arpeggios

We can create extensions to the arpeggios by adding notes to them just as we might extend the chords that they are derived from.

For example, any time we have an Am chord we can extend it to become an Am7. We do this just by adding the 7th note of the minor scale counting from A. So an Am7 arpeggio would have these notes:

```
        R  3  5  7
Am7:    A  C  E  G
```

On the guitar, we don't necessarily play the arpeggio notes in the same order. Sometimes it's easier and sounds just as good to play them in an order that's more comfortable on the guitar. For example, the diagram below shows a common way to to play an Am7 arpeggio on guitar. The notes are in this order: G C E A.

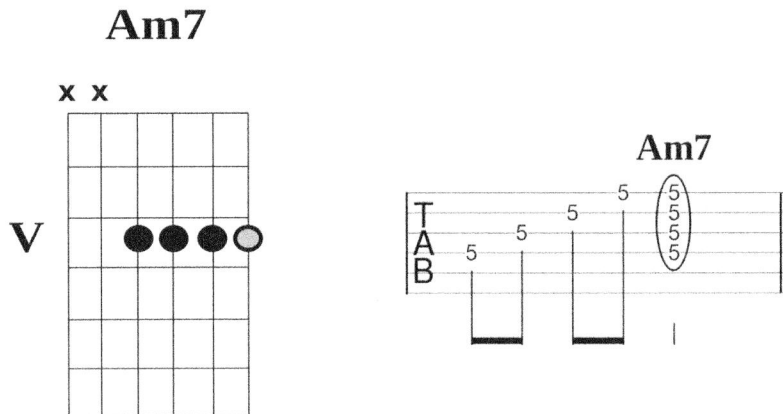

Am7

We could even extend that arpeggio further by adding a 9 to it. Now we have a very colourful sound. The chord in standard root position would be built like this:

```
        R   3   5   7   9
Am7:    A   C   E   G   B
```

But again, on the guitar we don't tend to play the notes in that order. Typically we would play them in this order: G C E A B.

Am9

Here is an exercise that includes licks with the Am9 arpeggio. Notice how interesting that 9 sounds. It's not in the pentatonic scale so it really stands out. It's slightly unexpected but somehow fits beautifully.

㉘

Arpeggios Outside the Scale

What if we have a chord that doesn't normally belong in a particular key? Songwriters do this quite often – a chord might be altered from major to minor or vice versa. The trick is this: you can outline any chord that happens to be in a song when it comes around. Remember, if the note is in the underlying chord, we can play it.

For example, in a modal song we might have these two chords: Am then D. In that case, I can play the Am arpeggio when the song is on Am, and I can play a D major arpeggio when the song switches to D.

If you're a fan of Santana's classic works you'll certainly have heard this chord sequence before. "Oye Como Va" uses this sequence extensively.

First, let's check what a D major arpeggio looks like.

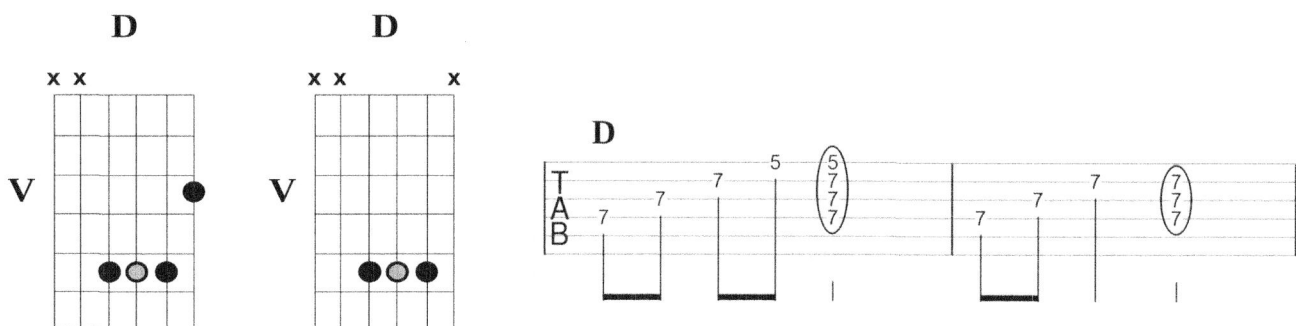

Next is a basic idea of how you can combine A minor pentatonic with a D major arpeggio. Notice how bright and interesting that D major sounds when compared with the Am. Measures 7 and 9 both have a D major arpeggio.

㉙

Jam Track 4 – Dorian Am to D

This jam track was designed to work with the previous exercise. It has only two chords: Am and D, one measure each.

> *This combination is a Dorian modal chord change. If that sounds like Greek to you, don't worry about it, you can still play it. There are many songs that have this minor to major chord change in them and they give us great opportunities to use both minor and major arpeggios in the same solo.*

Try to get the previous exercise up to speed with Jam Track 4, then try out your own lines using the arpeggios and chord shapes from this chapter.

Major Arpeggios in a Blues Form

In the blues, we are often playing A minor pentatonic (or the blues scale) over major chords. As we've discussed above, this theoretically should not sound good. If the underlying chords are all **major**, why would we play a **minor** scale over them? Part of the reason why it works is because the pentatonic scale only has five notes (plus the blue note) so we avoid some notes that will conflict.

We are still left with a minor 3rd in the scale while the major chord underneath has a major 3rd. But despite this conflict, it still just sounds great.

So in this case, the same rule applies: If the notes are in the chord underneath, we can use them, even if the notes are not in the scale we've chosen to play.

A Major chord arpeggio

Below is a common major chord arpeggio. Notice how it is also derived from the standard major bar chord shape (it's just the top half of it). Again, the big bar chord is too clunky for this use, so we're just taking the top three or four notes of it.

Jam Track 5 – 12-Bar Blues in A

This example starts with an A minor pentatonic blues lick in bar 1, then uses a D major arpeggio in bar 2. It goes back to A minor pentatonic in bar 3, but then switches to an A major arpeggio in bar 4.

Before you move on to Zone 2, it would be a good idea to review all the concepts we've covered so far. Make sure to practice these ideas as much as you can using the jam tracks. The next part of this book will explore all these ideas further and show you how to use them up the fretboard and to change keys.

Zone 2

Now that you are getting the hang of playing all these advanced techniques in Zone 1, it's time to start exploring further up the fretboard. I like to think of this as Zone 2 because it also has a root note that starts on the first finger. But in this case, the root note is on the A string.

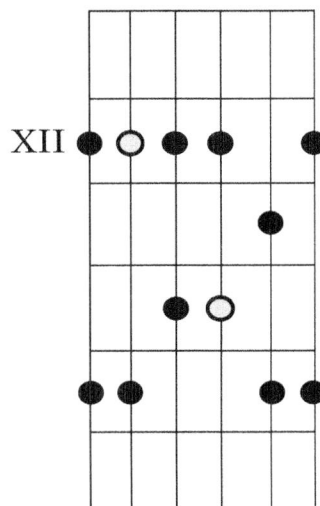

Pay careful attention to the diagram above that shows where that root note is on the A string. Even though we might memorize the entire shape starting from the E string, we need to remember that the root of the scale isn't on that string. This will help us to transpose the scale shape to other keys later on.

Sometimes I call this pentatonic shape the "First finger A string root" shape. That would mean that Zone 1 could also be referred to as the "First finger E string root." This becomes especially useful when you explore more pentatonic shapes that have a root under the 3rd finger.

Zone 2 basic licks in A minor

Let's try out some basic licks in A minor just to get our fingers used to that tricky B string in this shape. The fact that the notes on the B string are shifted up one fret can be challenging at first. But after a while you'll find it can inspire some really cool licks and fits comfortably in the hand if you use it the right way.

Zone 2 blue notes

You can't go wrong with the pentatonic shape on its own. But after a while it can sound just a little too simple. That's where the blue note comes in. Adding that touch of dissonance helps make your solos sound more dramatic.

So let's add the **blue note** to the Zone 2 Shape.

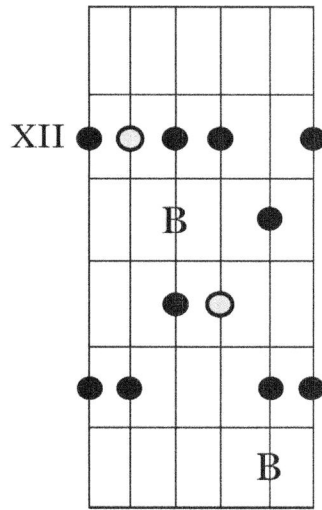

If we compare this shape to the Zone 1 shape, we can think of the blue notes as being in the same positions of the scale. We have just started one string up. So the scale still goes Root, note, note, blue-note, etc.

The blue note that is on the higher B string can be tricky to reach if you aren't careful which fingers you play the scale with. Below are a few common ways of dealing with it. All three of these fingerings might be used at different times, depending on the situation before or after the notes.

Left-hand fingering is written below the staff.

Common Notes to Bend in Zone 2

Now let's memorize where the common notes to bend in Zone 2 are. Potentially we can bend any note we want, but there are certain notes that will work well more often so it's worth learning them.

> *You might also notice that the common notes to bend also end up being notes that your third finger would typically play. That's no coincidence. It's much easier to bend a third-finger note than a first-finger. That's one reason why these are the notes that are most frequently bent in all our favourite classic rock songs.*

The following exercise shows the three most common bends in this shape. I've already placed them in the context of the Zone 2 scale so you can practice them.

The bend in the second measure is good for resolving phrases since we are bending a D note up to an E, the fifth of the scale. The fourth bar shows a bend from G resolving to the root, A.

Pre-Bends in Zone 2

As we discussed in Zone 1, there are a few ways we can bend a note. It's not always up-then-release. Another great effect is the pre-bend. To do that, bend the note before you pluck the string. Once the string is bent up, then pluck the string and release the string back in place.

In the following exercise, each line starts with a pre-bend and ends with a bend that spans the next bar-line.

Bending to the Blue Note

Have another look at where the blue note is in Zone 2 on the B string. It's just one fret above the common B-string bend in this shape. This means that we can bend this note either a whole step -- which is bending the D note to the pitch of a E -- or we can bend it up just a half step, to the sound of the blue note.

Double stops in Zone 2

Just like in Zone 1, there are some great double-stop licks that can add depth to your solos. And thankfully, they are still quite comfortable to play.

You can mix and match these double-stops as much as you like. Again, just try to remember where they are in the pentatonic shape.

Zone 2 in E minor

Thinking of your pentatonic shapes in terms of what finger it starts on is helpful for changing keys. If this Zone 2 shape is a "First finger on A string" shape, then all we must do to change keys is shift our first finger up or down the string to find the new key root.

For example, here's a diagram showing E minor pentatonic with the blue notes (the E Blues Scale). The shape is the same, but in this case we start on the 7th fret of the A string, for E.

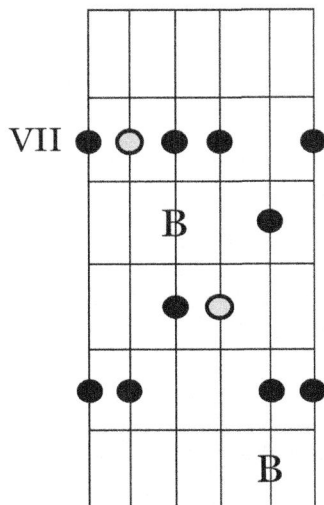

Pattern 1 Zone 2 – Up 4 back 1

The best way to develop your skills on the pentatonic shapes is to practice patterns. Not only do they help build muscle memory for the scale shapes, they also create musical habits that we can use when improvising, helping to avoid playing scale-wise too often.

Here is Pattern 1 – up 4, back one – but written for Zone 2. Remember, there is a reason why we aren't starting on the low 6th string. We want to get accustomed to starting on the root of the scale as it will help us to memorize the sound of the scale.

(36)

```
T
A
B 4/4
    7   10   7   9   7   9   7   9       7   9   8   10   8   10   7   10

T
A   10   7   10   8   10   8   9   7   9   7
B                                              9   7   9   7   10   7
```

Soloing Over Chords in Zone 2

Remember to consider not just the key of the song, but all the chords that are played when you're writing a solo or improvising. Make sure you know the chords in advance, and then listen for the harmonic changes as you play. Each chord change gives us a new opportunity to alter what we play. If you want to highlight a note from the chord underneath, you have to time it so that you play that note on the correct chord.

Highlight the roots of the chords in Zone 2

In this example we are going to solo over just two chords: Em and Am, two measures each. That's Im and IVm in the key of E minor. Here's the outline:

|Em |Em |Am |Am |

Using E minor pentatonic, we can solo over the first two bars playing any licks we like, but then aim for the root of the Am chord when we get to bar three.

Here's an exercise that will help you – and it may sound familiar. It's almost exactly the same as we did in Zone 1, but it's now transposed to the key of E minor and for Zone 2.

Notice that we hit the root of Am on the first beat of bar 3. Then in measure 5, the song returns to the Em chord so we hit the root E.

Then again, in bar 7 when the song switches to Am for the second time, we hit another A note, this time up the octave (A on the 10th fret of the B string).

Jam Track 6 – Em to Am

This simple jam track was designed for you to try out aiming for the roots of these two chords using the Zone 2 shape. Listen for the chord changes and play the roots on the changes. We don't have to do this every time, but it is a great trick for making your solos sound more melodic.

| Em | | Em | | Am | | Am | |

The Minor 3rd of the Im chord in Zone 2

In the last example we practised targeting the root notes of each chord. In this case, we're going to target the minor 3rd of the root chord, Em.

Just as we did in Zone 1, we can memorize where that note is based on the chord shape, or based on the pentatonic shape. So let's look at the Em chord shape:

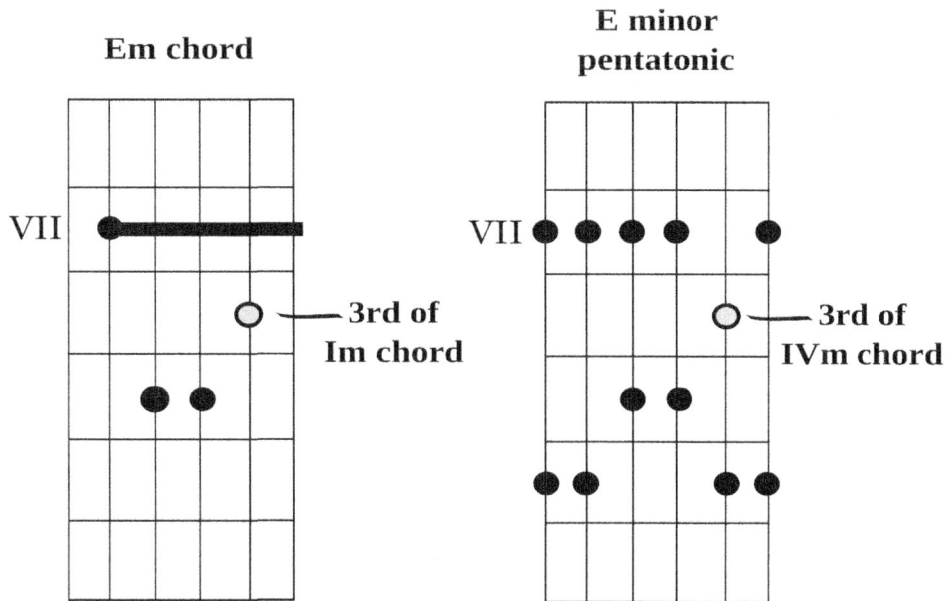

The first diagram above shows you where that 3rd is in the Em chord shape. Memorize where that note is because anytime a song is on an Em chord we can play that note. All we have to do is picture this chord shape, target that note, and just let it ring.

We can also picture where it sits against the minor pentatonic scale, as we see in the second diagram above.

38

Now go back to Jam Track 6 and try aiming for the minor 3rd of Em whenever you hear that root chord.

Chords for solos in Zone 2

Just like before, the best way to start playing chords in solos is to memorize where your I, IV and V chords are in this zone. These are the most common chords we find in popular music so it's the best place to start.

In this case, we're going to continue in the key of E minor. (The key of E Minor has only one sharp, but it happens to be a note we're not going to be concerned with now anyway.)

E Minor: E F# G A B C D

Therefore, the most common chords in the key of E minor are.

I: Em   IV: Am   V: Bm

The following charts show the standard bar chord forms. The second row illustrates the shortened chord forms that are more useful for solos. Notice how these "soloing chord forms" are the same shapes that we found in Zone 1, just in a different order.

Standard bar chord forms

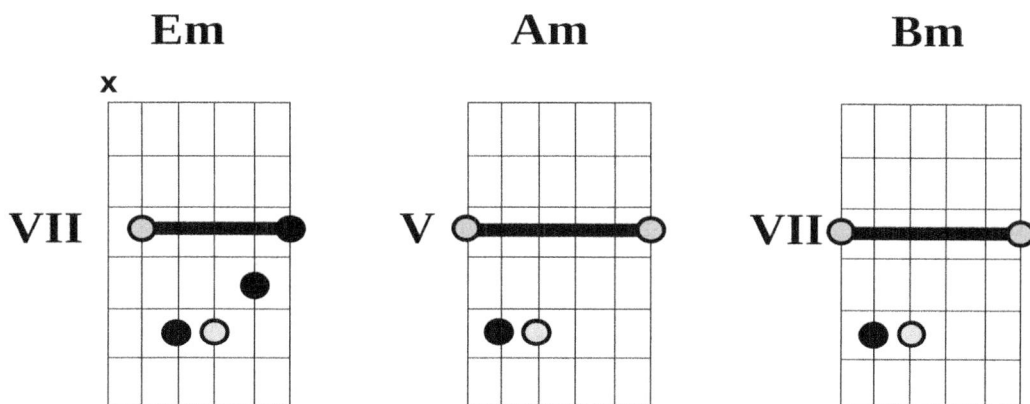

Soloing chord forms

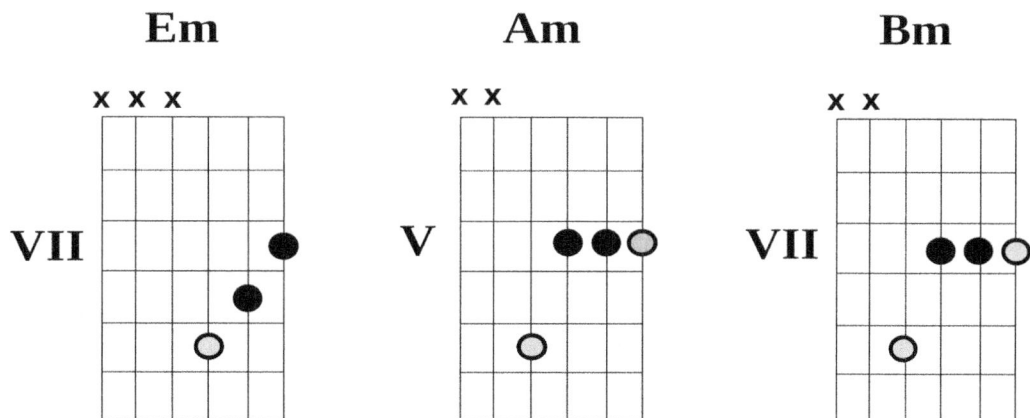

Zone 2 Chords Exercises

Let's do some exercises for these chord shapes to get accustomed to where they are positioned on the fretboard in relation to the Zone 2 Minor Pentatonic scale.

The IV minor chord in Zone 2

We can see that one of the challenges of the chords in this position is that the IV chord, the A minor in this case, is a few frets below and not quite as easy to reach. We could alternatively use another shape that would put this chord directly in the Zone 2 pentatonic shape without having to shift at all. It's a slightly more difficult shape, but it's worth exploring because once your fingers learn it, it's highly useful for both chords and arpeggios.

Additional IVm chord shapes

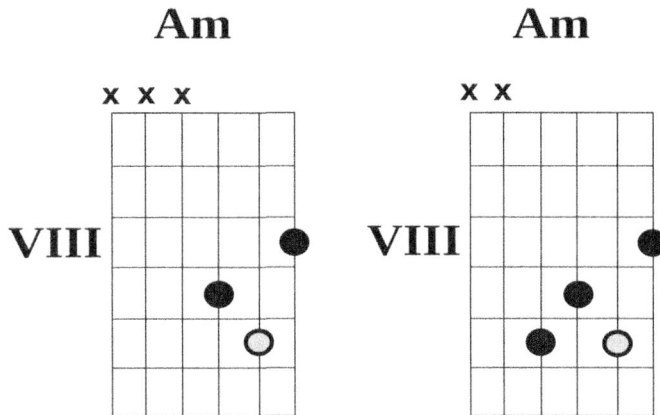

The first shape above is the easier version and we'll probably stick with that one for now. Generally when we want to grab a chord in a solo, we want to grab something that's quick and easy to visualize. (You might even recognize this shape as the standard open-position chord shape for Dm, it's just moved way up the fretboard.)

Try going back to the previous exercise and use this Am shape in bar 6 instead. You'll find you no longer need to jump down to the 5th fret to grab the chord. This shape is right there in Zone 2.

Zone 2 Chords Solo Exercise

Now it's time to play some licks and incorporate the chord shapes along with bends, pull-offs and melodic lines.

Zone 2 Runs

We don't want to feel stuck in a small part of the fretboard so now we're going to expand Zone 2 with some longer runs. Memorize these runs by practising them until you can play them smoothly and quickly.

Here is the first run which gives us a few notes below the root.

Remember to picture how the additional notes fit with the standard Zone 2 Minor Pentatonic scale. If you can picture it in your mind, you're less likely to get lost or make mistakes.

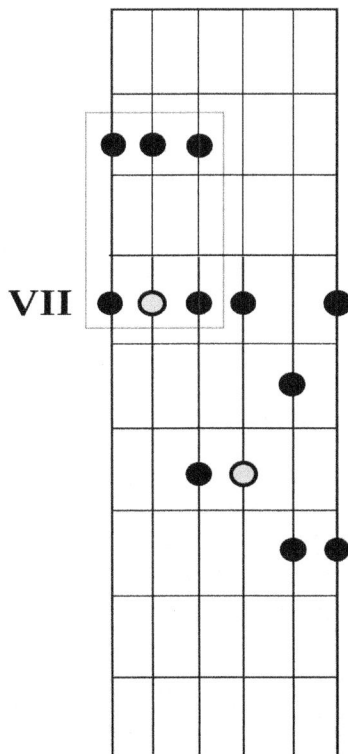

As an upper extension for the Zone 2 run we will just add one single note--the root that exists two frets up. Of course, there are other ways we can extend this shape, but keeping it simple at first is always a good idea. So for now, your Zone 2 upper extension just slides up to one final root note. That's a handy note to resolve with.

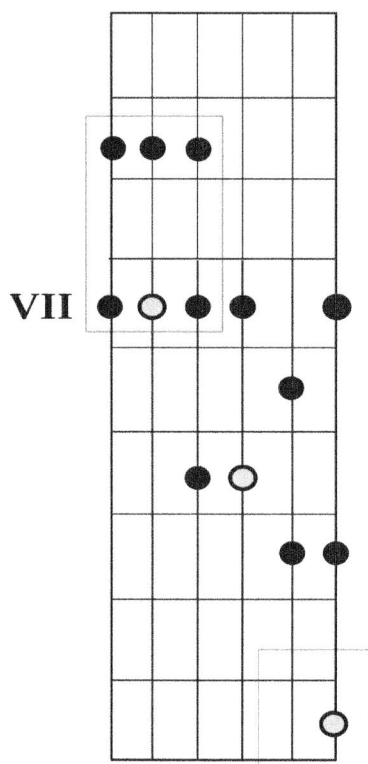

Let's play an exercise that runs from the bottom at the 5th fret all the way to the top at the 12th fret. That's a nice long run with a great resolve on the root at the end.

(42)

```
        sl.                                           sl.
T 4                          5   7——9    7    | 9              7——10——12
A 4         5    7                             |    8    10
B    5  7                                      |
```

```
   sl.                              sl.
T   12——10    7                   | 
A             10   8    9    7     | 7——5
B                           9      |        7    5
                                   |              7    5
```

Another way to play the complete run would be to play up to the 10th fret, then bend it a whole step up. If we bend that tenth fret up a whole step, we are bending to the root E. So now we could either play the extension up to E 12th fret. Or we can just bend to it.

(43)

```
                                                                    full
        sl.                                               7    (10)
T 4                          5    7——9    7    | 9              
A 4         5    7                             |    8    10
B    5  7                                      |
```

Double-Stop Bend and Touch

There is a very common lick in this shape that I like to call a double-stop bend, or sometimes I call it the bend-and-touch. It takes a little explaining on how to do this so here's a step-by-step description.

1) Use your third finger to bend the note. Don't release the note back down until step three.

73

2) While the second string is still bent up, use your pinky finger to "touch" or push down the 10th fret of the high E string. Your pick can then pick the high E string to play that note.

3) After you have plucked the high E string, your pick now strikes the second string again as you release the bend.

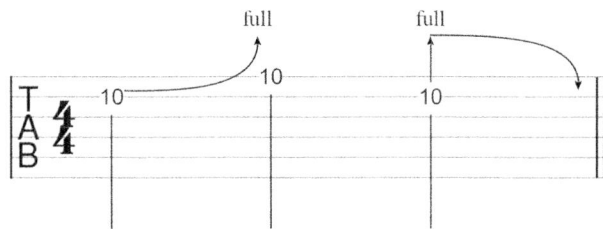

We can do this lick in other shapes easily enough. But this one in Zone 2 is in millions of songs. You can hear it in lots of the Rolling Stones' country inspired songs. It fits nicely in the 3rd finger in this shape and it just happens to sound great here.

Pattern 2 Zone 2 – Up 3 Back 1

Let's take a break from learning licks and practice the Zone 2 scale shape a bit more. It's true this is not the most fun part, but I can tell you with no exaggeration that practising these patterns is incredibly beneficial to becoming a skilled guitar player. It will build speed and accuracy.

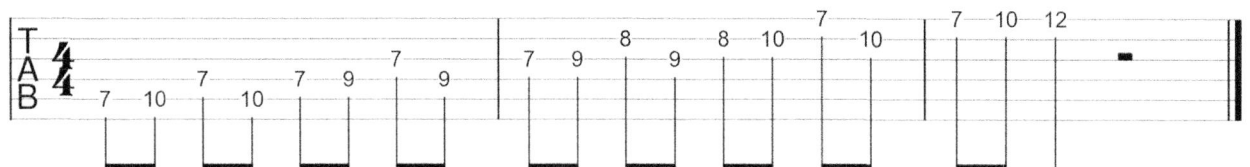

(46)

```
   10  7          7
T       10      7     10  8     8
A 4 4             9          9    7      7
B                           9      7   9  7
                                           10    7   10 7   7
                                                       10     10 7
```

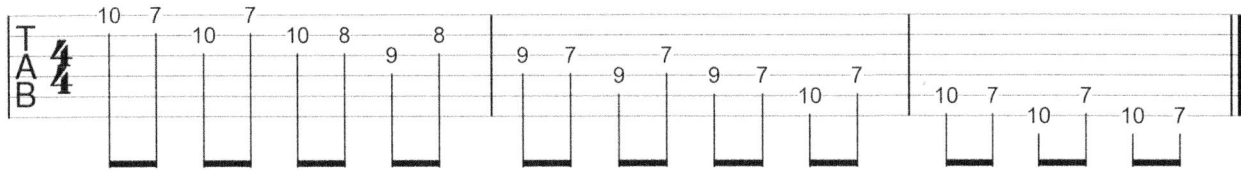

Zone 2 Minor Arpeggios

Since we have already learned the chord shapes for the I, IV and V chords in this zone, then it's easy enough to turn those shapes into arpeggios. Here are four arpeggio shapes to learn. The first is Em, then we have two different Am shapes based on the two chord shapes we learned, and finally the Bm arpeggio.

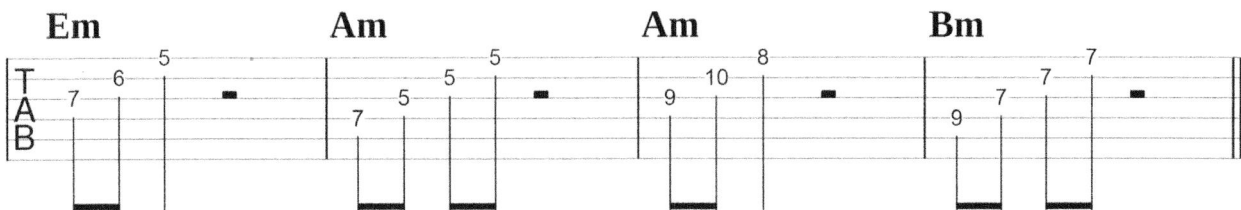

```
  Em              Am              Am              Bm
           5               5                8               7
T      6 5            5 5          10              7 7
A    7           7 5          9              7
B  7                              9
```

It can take some work before you can visualize how these arpeggio shapes fit alongside the pentatonic shape. As we can see, the Em arpeggio includes notes right out of the E minor pentatonic shape. But the Am arpeggio has a note that does not fit into the pentatonic shape. Remember, it doesn't matter if the note is not in the scale shape so long as it is in the chord being played at that moment.

Zone 2 Minor arpeggios exercise A

Here's an exercise to help your fingers get accustomed to playing these arpeggios alongside the pentatonic shape. With each chord we go up the arpeggio and then down the pentatonic. The last line includes the blue note as well.

Zone 2 Minor arpeggios exercise B

This exercise includes the other Am arpeggio shape and is written with some bends and other common licks.

In measures five and six we play the Am and Bm chords but we reach a finger to grab notes from the pentatonic shape to add to the chords. You can do this to any of these chords so long as you are adding notes from the key of the song.

Zone 2 Major V chord arpeggio

For a book that's all about the minor pentatonic, we have one final thing we haven't addressed yet: It's very common for a song in a minor key to alter the V chord and turn it into a major chord.

Remember that if we are in the key of E minor, then the standard I, IV and V chords are:

Em Am Bm

But it's also common to change the V chord into a major chord. This is known as Harmonic Minor. Thus we would have:

Em Am B

This is a good reminder for us to always be aware of what the chords are underneath whenever we are writing or improvising a solo. If we don't know the chords underneath, we can't effectively use these chord shapes or arpeggio shapes in our solos.

Here's what your three arpeggios would look like in this case. The first two are the same, but the V chord is now a major chord arpeggio.

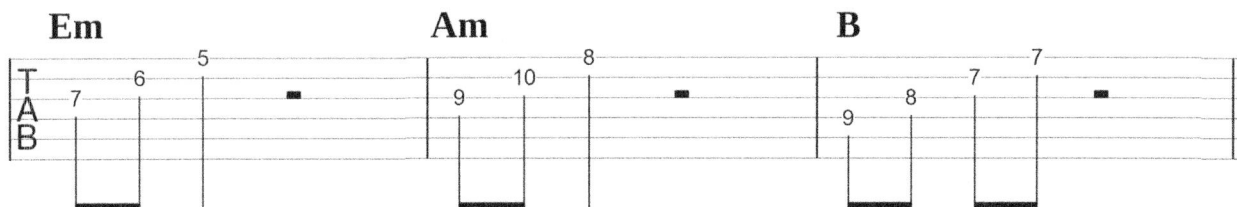

Soloing over the Major V Chord

When songs in a minor key have this altered V chord, it gives us some great opportunities to play very colourful notes. Think about it this way: whenever we have a chord that includes notes that are not in the scale, we can play those notes and add them to our solos.

Now let's try a longer example with some common licks in this key.

What's Next?

If you've managed to get all the way through this book and you can competently play all the exercises, then congratulations! It is my understanding that millions of music books are sold every year but most people don't make it though to the end of them. So you are one of the disciplined guitar players and you certainly deserve credit.

Of course there's always more to learn. Don't be discouraged by that – enjoy the process. No matter how good we get at music and guitar, there is always more to learn and that's one of the great things about it.

I hope to write and complete Book 2 soon! There's a whole new world of soloing using Major Pentatonic scales, and changing scales at will, which will be the focus of that book.

You can follow me on YouTube at:

https://www.youtube.com/GuitarLessonsVancouver

Join our Patreon guitar lessons group:

https://www.patreon.com/GuitarLessonsVancouver

Or visit my site at:

https://www.bluemorris.com

Printed in Great Britain
by Amazon

48648802R00044